ANTELOPE

Maddie Gibbs

PowerKiDS press.

New York

Published in 2011 by The Rosen Publishing Group, Inc.
29 East 21st Street, New York, NY 10010

First Edition

Editor: Amelie von Zumbusch
Layout Design: Greg Tucker

Photo Credits: Cover, pp. 7, 9, 11, 13, 15, 19 Shutterstock.com; p. 5 Anup Shah/Photodisc/Thinkstock; p. 17 Jupiterimages/Photos.com/Thinkstock; p. 21 Hemera/Thinkstock; p. 23 Tom Brakefield/Stockbyte/Thinkstock.

Library of Congress Cataloging-in-Publication Data

Gibbs, Maddie.
 Antelope / by Maddie Gibbs. — 1st ed.
    p. cm. — (Safari animals)
 Includes index.
 ISBN 978-1-4488-2507-3 (library binding) — ISBN 978-1-4488-2602-5 (pbk.) —
ISBN 978-1-4488-2603-2 (6-pack)
 1. Antelopes—Africa—Juvenile literature. I. Title.
 QL737.U53G525 2011
 599.64—dc22
                                    2010022370

Manufactured in the United States of America

CPSIA Compliance Information: Batch #WW11PK: For Further Information contact Rosen Publishing, New York, New York at 1-800-237-9932

CONTENTS

Africa is home to more than 70 kinds of antelope. These antelope are gemsbok.

Thomson's gazelles are another kind of antelope. They live on Africa's **grasslands**.

7

Springbok, such as the one here, often live in Africa's deserts.

9

This is an eland.
Eland are the largest
kind of antelope.

11

All male antelope have **horns**. Some female antelope have horns, too.

13

Male antelope use their horns to fight. They fight over land and females.

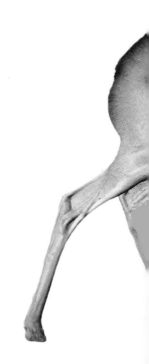

15

Most antelope live in groups, called **herds**.

17

Many antelope are good jumpers. Impalas can go 30 feet (9 m) in one jump!

19

Baby antelope are called **calves**. Calves drink their mothers' milk.

21

Adult antelope, such as this gerenuk, eat plants.

23

Words to Know

calf

grasslands

herd

horns

Index

Web Sites

Due to the changing nature of Internet links, PowerKids Press has developed an online list of Web sites related to the subject of this book. This site is updated regularly. Please use this link to access the list: www.powerkidslinks.com/safari/ante/